FLOODS

FLOODS

BY ANN ARMBRUSTER

A FIRST BOOK

Franklin Watts
A Division of Grolier Publishing
New York   London   Hong Kong   Sydney
Danbury, Connecticut

Cover and Interior Design Adaptation by Molly Heron

Photographs ©: American Red Cross: p. 47; AP/Wide World Photos: pp. 6, 44; Archive Photos: p. 24, chapter opener; Art Resource: pp. 9 (Anspach), 12 (Erich Lessing); The Bettmann Archive: pp. 29 inset, 52; Chauncey T. Hinman: p. 22 (both photos); Johnstown Area Heritage Association: p. 49; NASA: p. 20; NASA-Goddard Space Flight Center: p. 34; National Weather Service: p. 32 (both photos); NOAA: p. 29; Photo Researchers: pp. 19 (Mark Burnett), 31 (Martin Bond/SPL), 39 (Lowell J. Georgia), 40 (Adam Jones), 41 (George Holton), 45 (Joyce Photographics); Reuters/Bettmann: pp. 16, 26, 36, 53, 55; Royal Netherlands Embassy: p. 43; Superstock: cover, p. 2; UPI/Bettmann: p. 15; US Army Corps of Engineers: pp. 37, 57 (St. Louis District).

Library of Congress Cataloging-in-Publication Data

Armbruster, Ann.
    Floods / by Ann Armbruster.
        p. cm. — (A First book)
    Includes bibliographical references and index.
    Summary: Explains the various types of floods, provides a history of famous floods, and discusses the latest trends in flood prevention and control.
    ISBN 0-531-20239-9
    1. Floods—Juvenile literature. [1. Floods.] I. Title. II. Series.
    GB1399.A76 1996   96-14599 CIP AC
    551.48'9—dc20

CONTENTS

DOWN THROUGH THE AGES

Water is our most precious resource. No organism can live without it. This odorless, tasteless substance covers 70 percent of the earth's surface. We drink water, cook with water, bathe in water, sprinkle the lawn with water, and swim in water. It is essential to our survival.

Although water gives life, too much water—too soon—can take it away. When water rises and overflows onto normally dry land, we call this a flood. Floods happen when a river overflows its banks, a large wave hits a coastal area, a dam breaks, a storm produces a large amount of rain over a very short time, or the strong winds of a powerful ocean storm push a surge of water onto the coast. Floods occur in almost all parts of the world and kill more people than any other weather-related event.

A wall of water races through the streets of Putnam, Connecticut, during a flash flood on August 19, 1955. Though property damage from the Putnam flood was tremendous, no one was killed thanks to adequate warning and other flood safety measures.

For countless generations, people have settled on the rich land near rivers. The rivers provide excellent soil for crops, fine transportation, and an endless supply of water for daily use. These same rivers also fuel floods. A flood can sweep away crops, towns, and, worst of all, human lives. In most places, people return to rebuild their towns, accepting floods as a part of life near the water.

Modern technology helps us fight floods, but even today high waters frequently overwhelm our best efforts to contain them. Why do floods still take us by surprise? How can we predict them and prevent them? Should all floods be prevented?

FLOOD MYTHS

In earlier times, many people believed that floods were punishments sent by the gods. The theme of a great flood engulfing the earth is repeated in many myths and legends. In Greek mythology, Zeus, the king of the gods, disguised himself as a traveler and visited the earth. He discovered that people were wicked and deceitful. Zeus returned to Mount Olympus and said, "I must destroy the human race. They are not fit to live on the earth." He sent a tremendous flood that drowned almost all of the people.

Two good people, Deucalion and Pyrrha, were warned of the terrible flood. They built a large wooden boat, called an ark, and stocked it with provisions and herds of sheep and cattle. After the flood, the ark came to rest on Mount Parnassus, and Deucalion and Pyrrha gave thanks to the gods for their survival. Looking down from Olympus, Zeus pitied them and told them to scatter stones across the land. The stones thrown by Deucalion became men, and the stones thrown by Pyrrha became women. Another human race peopled the earth.

One of the best-known flood stories is recorded in the Book of Genesis in the Bible. According to this story, when God saw how wicked people had become, he decided to unleash a great flood upon the earth. He selected Noah, a

In this mosaic, Noah's family and the animals take refuge in the ark until the flood has subsided.

righteous man, to build an ark. In the ark, Noah gathered his family and two each of all living things. It rained for forty days and nights, causing a flood to cover the entire earth. Only the inhabitants of the ark survived. When the flood receded, Noah, his family, and the animals departed from the ark with God's blessing.

RIVER FLOODS

In the spring, melting snow and excessive rainfall can increase the amount of water in rivers, creeks, and other inland streams. Some of the water is absorbed by the soil; some is taken up by plants. The remaining water, called runoff, flows into nearby rivers and streams. The sudden influx of water can cause a river to rise. If a river rises so high that water overflows its banks, the result is a river flood.

A river is often bordered by flat land that is only slightly higher than the riverbed. When the water level rises, usually after a heavy rain, the river can flood the flat land beside it. This land, called the floodplain, may extend for miles on either side of the river. After a flood, the retreating water leaves behind mineral-rich soil, called silt, on the floodplain. As a result, floodplains tend to be very fertile, and throughout history people have settled in these areas to cultivate the soil and grow bountiful food. These periodic floods are both a blessing and a curse. They replenish the nutrients in the soil, contributing to the thriving agriculture, but they can also destroy communities and take many lives.

Periodic floods deposit mineral-rich silt on the banks of the Nile, allowing for lush vegetation. Beyond the reach of the river looms the barren desert.

THE NILE RIVER

The Nile River, which is the world's longest, flowing for 4,160 miles (6,695 km) through Africa into the Mediterranean Sea, is prone to these periodic floods. Yearly summer rains cause the river to overflow onto the flat land of the Egyptian desert, flooding the plains for several miles on each side of the river. Because of the floods, the Nile's floodplain is one of the most fertile farming regions in the world. It has nourished communities along the river since the time of the ancient Egyptians. Although the floods replenish the rich soil, they can also cause widespread damage. The fate of the communities inhabiting the Nile's banks has depended on the whims of the river. As an ancient Greek philosopher observed, "Egypt is the Nile and the Nile is Egypt." For centuries, when the river rose during flood season, the Egyptians held a religious festival in honor of the goddess Isis. They believed the river rose because Isis had dropped a tear into the water. A human sacrifice was often offered to please the goddess. Today, the Aswân High Dam regulates the flow of the Nile, preventing unusually high floods or shortages of water.

THE HUANG HO

The Huang Ho River in China also periodically overflows its banks. It is sometimes called the Yellow River because of the color of the water. As the 3,000-mile-long (4,830-km-long) river runs down from the Tibetan mountains toward the Yellow Sea, yellow soil is swept along, giving the river water its color. This river is also known as "China's Sorrow" because it has produced more devastating floods and killed more people than any other river in the world. In 1887, the Huang Ho caused one of the world's worst natural disasters. Over 50,000 square miles (130,000 sq km) of land were flooded. Two million people lost their homes, about 900,000 people died in the high waters, and a million more were lost to disease and starvation soon after the flood.

THE MISSISSIPPI RIVER

This principal river of the United States flows generally south from Lake Itasca in Minnesota to the Gulf of Mexico. With the Missouri River, the Mississippi River forms the world's third-longest river system, running about 2,470 miles (3,975 km), though the length is constantly changing. Fed by other rivers,

On November 4, 1966, after 19 inches (48 cm) of rain drenched the area, a terrible flood bore down on Florence, Italy. Though human casualties were remarkably few, the city's priceless collection of art and literature was severely damaged. Up to 20 feet (6 m) of water and sludge swamped churches and museums, ruining books, sculptures, and paintings, many of which had been stored in basements and other low-lying spaces. After the flood, hundreds of students and art experts from all over the world flocked to Florence to restore the city. Thanks to their efforts and the courage of the Florentines, much of the damage has been undone. In this photograph, Brother Bonaventura stands in the courtyard of the Cathedral of Santa Croce several months after the flood. He points to an iron well that was covered by water up to the cross at its top.

14

The sense of humor of some Genevieve, Missouri, residents, could not be dampened by the severe floods of 1993. Pictured here, flooded South Main Street was dubbed "Lake S. Main."

such as the Ohio River, the Mississippi has a history of devastating floods.

In 1993, severe flooding again struck the Mississippi valley. Heavy rains in 1992 left the soil saturated through the winter. When spring rains began, the soil couldn't absorb more moisture. From April through June of 1993, 16.13 inches (40.97 cm) of rain fell in the upper Mississippi valley. This was the wettest spring since 1885.

Continued torrential rain through June and July caused 1,100 levees to fail. Tributaries of the Mississippi, and the river itself, began to flood. During that summer, local citizens and volunteers filled 26 million sandbags with more than 927 million pounds (420 million kg) of sand.

Despite these heroic efforts, the floods killed 47 people, damaged or destroyed more than 40,000 buildings, and flooded about 15,000 square miles (40,000 sq km) in the Mississippi River basin. President Bill Clinton declared 300 counties disaster areas, and total flood damage was estimated at $12 billion. Destruction from the flood was tremendous, but most people are thankful it wasn't much worse. Modern forecasts warned inhabitants of the area of the floods well in advance, giving them time to protect themselves and some property.

Throughout the Midwest, thousands of people have returned to rebuild their homes and their lives. Jerry Daugherty, a flood victim in St. Charles County, Missouri, said, "We never thought of leaving. It's our home. It's our heritage. It's our culture. And the river, once it gets in your blood, it's there." Despite this sentiment, the area was hit so hard by floods that only a fraction of the 3,500 people forced from their homes in St. Charles County have returned.

FLASH FLOODS

Many river floods are the result of days of heavy rain. The river may rise gradually, giving nearby communities plenty of time to prepare for the imminent flood. Other river floods strike with little or no warning. These are called flash floods, and they usually follow a very heavy rain or sudden snowmelt. The most severe flash floods often occur in mountainous regions, where floodwaters from small rivers and streams can tumble down gulches and canyons, inundating towns and roads below.

On the evening of June 14, 1990, a disastrous flash flood struck Shadyside, a community on the Ohio River in southeastern Ohio. About 3 to 4 inches (8 to 10 cm) of rain fell between 8:30 P.M. and 9:30 P.M., causing two local creeks to overflow. The resulting flood produced a wall of water up to 30 feet (9 m) high by 9:30 P.M. The flood killed 26 people and caused 6 to 8 million dollars in damage.

Rescue workers search for victims of a flash flood in Shadyside, Ohio.

Hurricane Florence from the point of view of Space Shuttle astronauts on November 14, 1994: the eye is clearly visible in the center of the pinwheeling mass of clouds.

3

COASTAL FLOODS

Coastal floods occur when powerful storms or unusually high waves or tides push ocean water onto the shore. This kind of flooding is most common in coastal areas that lie below sea level.

STORM FLOODS

Any powerful storm over open water can cause coastal flooding, especially if it strikes at high tide. The high winds associated with the storm are responsible for driving waves onto low-lying areas adjacent to the water. The most devastating flooding is usually caused by tropical storms—a special kind of storm that forms only at certain times of year over warm ocean water.

A hurricane, called a typhoon in the western Pacific, is the most severe tropical storm, with strong swirling winds and heavy rains. Seen from the air, a hurricane looks like a large mass of pinwheeling clouds with a small hole in the center.

This hole, called the eye, is the low-pressure center

around which a hurricane rotates. The eye may be from 25 to 50 miles (40 to 80 km) in diameter, and within this area the weather is often very tranquil, with light winds and fair skies. However, the area just outside the eye, the eye wall, is usually the most violent part of the hurricane, with winds that can gust in excess of 200 miles per hour (320 km/hr). When a hurricane makes landfall, these winds can drive huge amounts of water into the shoreline. This is called the storm surge, and the height of the incoming water varies with the strength of the storm and the shape of the coastline. In almost all landfalling hurricanes, the storm surge is the leading cause of death and destruction.

In 1969, Hurricane Camille touched down at Gulfport, Mississippi, with winds up to 210 miles per hour (338 km/hr). The storm surge along the coast was 24.2 feet (7.4 m) above normal sea level, the highest in United States history. Waves three stories high destroyed homes and cars. In the town of Pass Christian, Mississippi, floodwaters damaged the homes of all 4,000 residents. More than 100 people were killed in the Gulf Coast area alone. In the wake of Camille, 255 people died with 68 more reported missing.

Powerful tropical storms have been even more devastating in other areas of the world, especially Bangladesh, a country just east of India. Much of Bangladesh lies near sea level,

Ignoring evacuation warnings, residents of the beachfront Richelieu Apartments decided to have a "hurricane party" during Hurricane Camille. As shown in these before and after photographs, the storm surge completely leveled the apartment complex. Of the 24 people inside, only one survived. She was found in a treetop 5 miles (8 km) away.

Extratropical storms can be just as damaging as tropical storms.
This California house sinks into a storm-tossed sea.

so tropical storms from the Bay of Bengal to the south can cause large portions of the nation to be inundated. At times, 70 percent to 80 percent of the country has been underwater in the aftermath of a severe storm surge. In 1970, a tropical cyclone from the Bay of Bengal killed 300,000 people in Bangladesh. A similar storm in 1991 killed about 150,000 people and caused billions of dollars in damage.

Storms that are not of tropical origin are called extratropical storms. They are much more common and usually less powerful than tropical storms, but these storms can also cause serious coastal flooding. Areas of the West Coast of the United States can be bombarded by powerful extratropical storms that sweep in off the Pacific Ocean. Sometimes, a weather pattern can persist for days or weeks, driving a seemingly endless string of storms into the West Coast. These storms can cause widespread flooding from California to Washington.

In January 1996, high winds, heavy rains, and melting snow caused severe flooding along the West Coast. Thousands of people were evacuated from their homes. President Clinton visited the area and declared 24 counties in California national disaster areas. The floods caused about 300 million dollars in damage and 11 deaths. In February 1996, severe flooding again struck the West Coast, this time focusing on Washington and Oregon. President Clinton again visited the area and promised millions of dollars in federal aid.

The East Coast of the United States gets its share of coastal floods from extratropical ocean storms, too. The most famous of these storms is the northeaster (or nor'easter). Northeasters are powerful storms that form along the East Coast in the late fall, winter, and early spring. These storms

In December 1992, one of the most powerful northeasters on record battered the Northeast. High surf and strong winds pummelled this coastal section of New York City as several feet of snow fell inland.

can cause torrential rains and very heavy snowfalls. As a northeaster moves north along the East Coast from North Carolina to Maine, the winds ahead of the storm usually become northeasterly. This is what gives the storm its name. These winds frequently become very strong, occasionally gusting over 100 miles per hour (160 km/hr) in the most powerful northeasters. The combination of heavy precipitation, high winds, and huge waves can cause severe flooding and beach erosion. To make matters worse, some northeasters linger offshore for several days, battering the coastline for a prolonged period of time.

Sometimes, coastal floods strike areas that are several miles inland. This happens along rivers that drain into oceans, seas, or bays. Unlike most rivers, which flood after heavy rains, these rivers flood because of storm surges sent upstream by strong ocean storms over the nearby open waters.

London, England, is one area where this kind of flooding occurs. The source of floods in London is the Thames River, which is close enough to the seacoast to be affected by tides and storms over the North Sea. When a powerful storm over the nearby North Sea sends a surge of water up the Thames into London, the river can overflow, especially during abnormally high tides. Such a flood occurred in 1953, when the Thames rose over 3 feet (90 cm) above an already high tide, causing disastrous floods in southeastern England.

TSUNAMIS

A tsunami (often called a tidal wave, though it has nothing to do with tides) is a very large ocean wave caused by an underwater earthquake or volcanic eruption. A major disturbance on the ocean floor causes the seabed to shift suddenly, producing incredibly energetic waves that can travel at speeds up to 500 miles per hour (800 km/hr). In the open ocean, the waves are not very high at all, rising and falling only about 1 to

2 feet (30 to 60 cm). As a result, tsunamis usually pass unnoticed under ships at sea. These waves, however, are extremely long—the distance between crests can be as much as 125 miles (200 km). Though harmless out at sea, a tsunami transforms into a killer wave as it nears the shore. As it approaches the coast, a tsunami travels into shallower waters. At this point, it begins to be influenced by friction from the sea floor, and it slows down dramatically. The speed of a land-falling tsunami can decrease very rapidly from near 500 miles per hour (800 km/hr) to about 15 miles per hour (25 km/hr). This energy is not lost, however; it is transferred into the height of the wave. A tsunami can increase in height from 2 feet (60 cm) to more than 100 feet (30 m) in only a few minutes. As it strikes the coast, sometimes without warning, it often produces severe flooding and destruction.

The biggest recorded tsunami resulted from volcanic explosions that destroyed the island of Krakatoa, Indonesia, in 1883. Waves as high as 135 feet (41 m) assaulted villages on the coasts of nearby islands, killing at least 36,000 people. Another violent tsunami hit the Hawaiian Islands on April 1, 1946. Giant waves, caused by an earthquake in the North Pacific, ripped up coral reefs, battered homes, and destroyed the sandy beaches. Tsunamis up to 40 feet (12 m) high pounded Hilo, Hawaii, killing 179 people and causing 25 million dollars in damage. This tragedy sparked the development of the Seismic Sea Wave Warning System (SS-WWS), which has since become the Tsunami Warning System (TWS). This warning system consists of sensors that monitor disturbances on the ocean floor. Areas in the path of a tsunami can now usually be warned before the wave strikes.

*(Top) A massive wave over-
takes a Hilo resident during
the 1946 tsunami disaster.
(Inset) Part of Hilo, Hawaii,
after the tsunami.*

FLOOD CONTROL

The only way to completely avoid floods is to live where there is no danger of high waters. This, however, would deprive people of fertile farmland, industrial growth, aquatic recreation, and many other benefits of living near water. In the United States, it is estimated that 12 percent of the population live in flood-prone areas. As a result, scientists and engineers must continually search for better methods of flood control.

FORECASTING FLOODS

The first step in controlling the effects of floods is to be able to predict them and understand what causes them. Forecasting floods is the role of hydrologists (scientists who study water) and meteorologists (scientists who study weather conditions). The information they provide the public saves lives and property.

Many of the devices scientists use to predict floods are very simple. For example, they use rain gauges to measure the amount of rain that has fallen in a particular area, and

River gauges indicate the water level of a river. Here, the River Severn, in Gloucestershire, United Kingdom, is above flood stage.

river gauges to monitor changes in water levels. The point at which the water level is high enough to begin flooding is called the flood stage. Many bridges and piers along flood-prone rivers are equipped with instruments that set off loud alarms when a river is near flood stage. This alarm warns nearby communities of an impending flood.

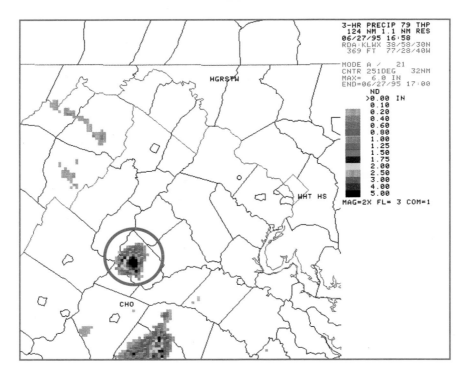

3-HR PRECIP 79 THP
124 NM 1.1 NM RES
06/27/95 16:58
RDA:KLWX 38/58/30N
369 FT 77/28/40W

MODE A / 21
CNTR 251DEG   32NM
MAX=   6.0 IN
END=06/27/95 17:00

ND
>0.00 IN
0.10
0.20
0.40
0.60
0.80
1.00
1.25
1.50
1.75
2.00
2.50
3.00
4.00
5.00

MAG=2X FL= 3 COM=1

HGRSTW

WHT HS

CHO

STM ID	AZ	RAN	TVS	MESO	HAIL	DBZM	HGT	VLOW	STM TOP	FCST	MVMT	MW VOL
52	205	88	NO	NO	NEG	51	10.2	24	29.18	140	9	1876
89	230	53	NO	NO	NEG	55	15.8	24	25.89	140	1	1187
50	295	73	NO	NO	NEG	40	7.9	27	14.58	193	11	183

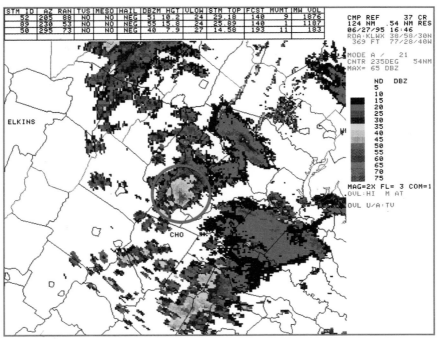

CMP REF   37 CR
124 NM .54 NM RES
06/27/95 16:46
RDA:KLWX 38/58/30N
369 FT 77/28/40W

MODE A / 21
CNTR 235DEG   54NM
MAX= 65 DBZ

ND DBZ
5
10
15
20
25
30
35
40
45
50
55
60
65
70
75

MAG=2X FL= 3 COM=1
OVL:HI M AT

OVL U/A:TV

ELKINS

CHO

Some weather-forecasting instruments are more sophisticated. They are used to monitor current weather conditions, issue short-term forecasts, and to predict weather conditions days in advance. Doppler radar is one of the most important of these devices, especially for predicting floods. Information gathered by Doppler radar is used to generate images showing any precipitation falling within range of the radar site, as well as the motion and the intensity of this precipitation. Doppler radar can also accurately estimate the amount of precipitation that has fallen over a period of time. Today, almost all areas of the United States are within range of a Doppler radar site. Another important tool is satellite imagery. Earth-orbiting satellites with special cameras take pictures of cloud tops. These images show meteorologists the movement and development of storms.

Perhaps the most sophisticated devices that meteorologists and hydrologists use to predict weather are computer models. These models are computer programs that gather

These Doppler radar images show the amount and intensity of rainfall that led to a flash flood in Madison County, Virginia, on June 27, 1995. The top image shows the amount of rain that fell in a three-hour period while thunderstorms swept through the area. By matching the colors on the map with its key on the right, a forecaster can tell that more than 5 inches (13 cm) of rain has fallen in the area covered by black dots (in circled area). The bottom image shows the intensity of the thunderstorms at a particular moment in time. The red and yellow areas indicate the most intense storms. By viewing a sequence of these images, a forecaster can track the paths of the storms. Note that the area of greatest intensity (in circled area) corresponds with the area of greatest precipitation in the top image.

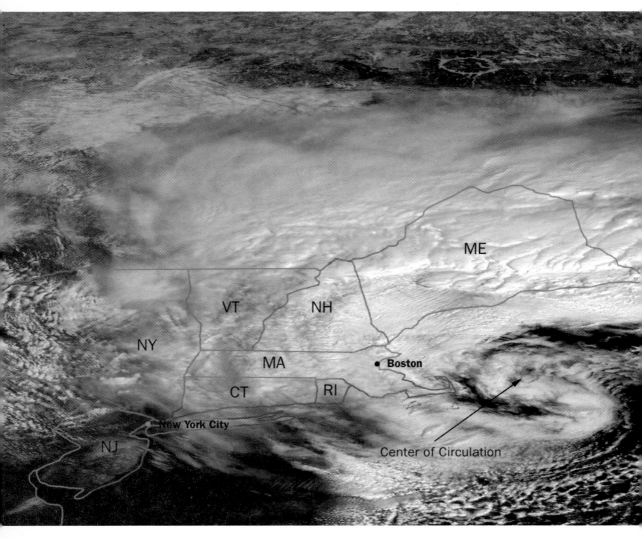

ME

VT

NH

NY

MA

• Boston

CT

RI

New York City

Center of Circulation

NJ

This satellite image shows an intense northeaster spinning off the coast of Cape Cod, Massachusetts. Extratropical storms like this one can cause flooding just as severe as the flooding caused by many tropical storms. Although there is a clear center of circulation, an extratropical storm does not have an eye like a hurricane.

information from all other meteorological tools and predict what will happen days in advance. The computer models do this by simulating actual weather phenomena.

In 1961, the United States Weather Bureau installed in Fort Worth, Texas, its first computer specifically designed for river flood forecasts. This computer model can generate about 250 local forecasts for rivers and streams along the Gulf Coast in just a few minutes.

The National Weather Service issues a series of watches and warnings to alert the public to flood dangers:

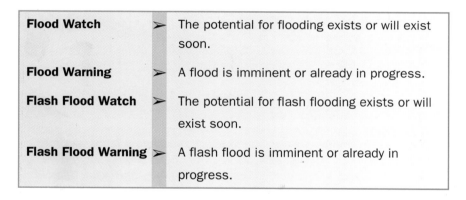

Flood Watch	➤	The potential for flooding exists or will exist soon.
Flood Warning	➤	A flood is imminent or already in progress.
Flash Flood Watch	➤	The potential for flash flooding exists or will exist soon.
Flash Flood Warning	➤	A flash flood is imminent or already in progress.

These warnings appear in forecasts issued directly by the National Weather Service and in local television and radio weather forecasts

FIGHTING FLOODS

Humans cannot control the weather that produces floods, but the geography of a flood-prone area can be altered to alleviate some flood dangers. People have taken such measures to protect themselves for hundreds of years. Native Americans,

Hundreds of volunteers use sandbags to reinforce a levee along the Mississippi River on August 4, 1993. They hope to prevent the rising river from flooding the downtown area of Prairie du Rocher, Illinois.

for instance, built mounds for places of refuge during a flood. Some flood prevention techniques are more sophisticated today, but almost all hinge on one of two simple principles: holding back floodwaters or raising inhabited areas above flood stage. These methods are not always successful, but when properly implemented, they can stabilize the fair-weather friendship between a waterside community and its body of water.

Openings in this levee allow rising water to be diverted from the Mississippi River (left) into a floodway (right) during a 1973 flood. This lowers the water level in the main river and protects towns downstream.

FIGHTING RIVER FLOODS

Levees—strong embankments made of dirt, sandbags, or concrete—have been built along riverbanks since ancient times to hold back floodwaters. By raising and strengthening the banks of a river, levees can make a river much less likely to flood.

Natural levees develop along the banks of rivers due to the buildup of silt and sediment deposited by repeated floods. When natural levees fail, stronger artificial levees are needed. At one time, the land around the lower Mississippi was considered one of the world's most dangerous flood zones. To provide some degree of control over floods along the unpredictable Mississippi River, huge levees have been built at key points, and smaller levees confine much of the southern part of the river. Many levees allow some floodwater to overflow into floodways. These channels divert excess water away from populated areas and then guide it back into the river past the danger zone.

A dam is another type of earthen or concrete flood barrier. It is built across a river or stream to control the flow of water. The water collects behind the dam to form an artificial lake called a reservoir. A portion of reservoir water is purified and stored in large tanks for drinking water; the remaining water may be used for crop irrigation or to run generators that produce electricity. A well-designed dam prevents a river from reaching extreme stages of drought or flood. Water in the reservoir is stored for use in times of drought, and runoff from heavy rains is released into the river in a slow, controlled manner.

Dams are enormous construction projects. In 1936, construction of Hoover Dam was completed. The dam rises 726 feet (221 m) above the Colorado River between Nevada and Arizona, and it consists of enough concrete to pave a two-lane highway from New York to San Francisco. It provides flood control, hydroelectric power, and water for irrigation as far away as southern California. The dam's reservoir, Lake Mead, is a popular tourist attraction.

In the past century, dams and levees have given us much more control over potential floods. However, severe floods can sometimes overwhelm even these artificial barriers. Alternate methods of flood control must also be practiced.

Contour farming is one of these methods. Farmers plow along the contours of a hillside, across the slope, instead of plowing up and down the slope. The furrows—the long, narrow grooves made in the ground by a plow—retain water that flows over them, slowing the progress of floodwaters.

Hoover Dam and its reservoir, Lake Mead

Another method, called terracing, is often used on steep hills to prevent valuable topsoil from being washed away by heavy rain. The steep land is converted into a series of large steps called terraces. The flat surfaces of the terraces absorb more water and produce less runoff than the original slope, so the risk of flooding and soil erosion is lessened. In addition,

Contour farming is practiced on this farm in eastern Washington. The furrows follow the contours of the hills.

trees and plants are placed on hillsides to help the soil absorb the water and hold the soil in place.

Diversion channels can sometimes prevent floods, too. This method involves changing the natural course of a river by rerouting the water through an artificial channel. The new channel guides the water in another direction, lowers the

Terraces on hillsides near the Ganges River in India

water level, and lessens the danger of flooding in an inhabited area. Diversion channels have been built at key points along the Mississippi River and the Sacramento River in California.

FIGHTING COASTAL FLOODS

Some inhabited areas near the seashore lie at or below sea level. These areas are frequently at risk for widespread flooding. Many low-lying coastal communities have built strong embankments along the coastline to hold back the sea. These barriers are called dikes, and some countries depend on them to keep highly populated areas free from floods.

The Netherlands is one of these countries. About 27 percent of the Netherlands lies below sea level, and about 20 percent of the country has actually been reclaimed from the North Sea. This has been accomplished by holding back the sea with dikes and draining the enclosed area with pumps. These areas that were formerly covered by the sea are called polders, and some of the Netherlands' most populated areas are located on them. Without the dikes and dams that protect the Netherlands, disastrous flooding would be a frequent occurrence, and the North Sea would take back the polders. Most of the time, the dikes have prevented floods, but like any flood barrier, they have failed on occasion. On February 1, 1953, a ferocious storm and an unusually high tide caused the catastrophic flooding of 625 square miles (1,619 sq km) in the southwestern portion of the country. Water covered almost one-eighth of the country's total area, and about

This dike near Terneuzen, the Netherlands, is overwhelmed by the February 1953 gales.

The 1953 flood overtakes the village of Oude Tonge. The disaster killed three hundred people here.

The Thames flood barrier: notice that the station on the far right is raising one of the gates.

1,800 people were killed. Since then, an improved system of dikes and dams has been implemented to keep the region secure.

Barriers have also been built in London to help prevent floods caused by storm surges that travel up the Thames River from the North Sea. These barriers are especially important in London because the Thames is rising at the rate of 3 feet (90 cm) per century, while the city is sinking at the rate of 1 foot (30 cm) per century. This is particularly alarming because London's underground train system and docks are built at or below sea level. Work began on London's tidal barrier system in 1974, and it was completed in 1982 at a cost of about $100 million. The Thames barrier consists of nine piers built in a line across the river. Between the piers are 10 steel gates, 200 feet (60 m) across, that can be closed to hold back floodwaters.

Many coastal floods are impossible to prevent; the forces that drive the water into the shore are too powerful to combat. Instead, authorities concentrate on warning systems, evacuation plans, and zoning restrictions to protect coastal residents.

WHEN THE BARRIERS FAIL

Flood barriers are not expected to work all the time. Flood control specialists accept the fact that with current technology, we cannot completely eliminate the risk of unwanted flooding. Experts cannot agree, however, on whether flood barriers may actually increase the severity of floods in some cases. This controversy raged during the 1993 floods along the Mississippi. Many experts argued that the levees that failed unleashed more destructive floods than would have occurred without the barriers.

Probably the most infamous example of a catastrophe caused by the failure of an artificial barrier is the Johnstown flood. In 1889, Johnstown, Pennsylvania, was a bustling steel-making town of 30,000 people nestled in the Allegheny Mountains. About 16 miles (26 km) away, the South Fork Dam held back the waters of the Little Conemaugh River. It was one of the nation's largest earthen dams, and it was known to be in poor condition. Behind the dam was a huge reservoir, Lake Conemaugh, which could hold 5 billion gallons (200 million liters) of water.

Main Street after the Johnstown flood

The South Fork Dam had been built by the state of Pennsylvania, but in 1889 it was sold to promoters who converted the area into a country club. An earlier flood had damaged portions of the dam, but the new owners showed little concern about this matter. Patchy repairs were made, but many problems were ignored.

On the morning of May 31, 1889, after two days of heavy rain, floodwaters in Johnstown reached a height of 5 feet (1.5 m). The waters of Lake Conemaugh reached almost to the top of the dam. At around 3:10 P.M., the dam burst with a deafening roar. One observed exclaimed, "When I witnessed this, I exclaimed, 'God have mercy on the peoples below.'"

A gigantic avalanche of destruction roared down the narrow valley toward Johnstown. Twenty million tons of water smashed through the towns of Woodvalle, Mineral Point, and East Conemaugh, destroying everything in sight. At some points the wall of water was 50 feet (15 m) high.

The flood hit Johnstown at 4:10 P.M. One reporter who escaped to a high hill wrote, "In an instant the deserted streets became black with people running for their lives . . . the flood came and licked them up with one eager and ferocious lap." Hundreds of people died as floodwaters reached a depth of 30 feet (9 m).

The roaring wreckage of humans, houses, and debris was stopped by the thick stone arches of Stone Bridge. This railroad bridge, which spanned the river, held back the roaring water, but a terrible load of debris began piling up. In some places the tangled mess covered 20 square blocks and reached a height of about 70 feet (21m). At the same time, backed-up floodwaters rebounded off the bridge and surged back into the city.

At six o'clock that same evening, the mass of rubble burst into flames. Live coals from overturned stoves had

Wreckage piled against Stone Bridge

caught fire with the oil and gas in the water. An observer who viewed the pandemonium said, "It reminded me of a lot of flies on flypaper, struggling to get away, with no hope."

The Johnstown flood killed 2,220 people with 99 families completely eliminated. Nevertheless, the survivors rebuilt their town and the tragedy slowly faded, though it has never been forgotten. One of the rescue workers stayed for five months. She was Clara Barton, the founder of the Red Cross, an organization committed to disaster relief.

Because the city lies in a valley near two rivers, Johnstown is still prone to floods. In spite of river walls and other flood control projects, the Conemaugh River flooded again in 1977, causing the death of 85 residents.

5

FLOOD RESCUE AND SAFETY

When a flood strikes, people overtaken by the high waters must be pulled to safety. People stranded on the upper floors of houses, in trees, or in other high areas also must be rescued. Local organizations, the police and fire departments, and other civil defense teams often work together, using boats and helicopters in their rescue missions. Local church groups and numerous volunteers unite to seek food, clothing, and shelter for the flood victims. During severe floods, the Red Cross, National Guard, and Coast Guard frequently participate in the disaster-relief effort.

Search-and-rescue operations must be conducted to locate the dead and injured. Bodies must be identified and buried and the injured transported to hospitals. Workers from utility companies must restore electric power, fuel supplies, and telephone service. Drinking water must be tested and damaged property restored. Most flood-stricken towns share one common obstacle—mud, tons and tons of it. The chocolate-colored mud may be mixed with industrial waste, pesticides, and raw sewage. Flooded areas are usually a muddy, stinking mess to clean up.

A man is a dog's best friend as two National Guardsmen use a special device to pull a grateful golden retriever to safety during a July 1994 flood in Albany, Georgia.

Two members of the Monte Rio Fire Rescue team evacuate residents of the northern California town during a flood on January 10, 1995.

IN THE EVENT OF A FLOOD

If you are ever faced with a flood emergency, you'll want to remember these safety suggestions offered by the Federal Emergency Management Agency (FEMA) and the National Weather Service:

- Seek high ground immediately.
- Stay away from flooded areas and areas prone to flooding.

- Avoid camping on low ground near rivers or streams.
- If near a river, find out where high ground is located.
- If floodwaters invade your home, move to the second floor or to the roof.
- If floodwaters have not yet invaded your home, turn off all utilities at the main power switch.
- Fill bathtubs, sinks, and jugs with clean water.
- Dispose of any contaminated food. Boil all tap water before you use it.
- Don't attempt to walk through floodwaters that are more than knee deep.
- Don't drive through flooded areas.
- If you are in a car surrounded by rising water, leave the car and seek safety on higher ground.

Following these safety guidelines can go a long way toward protecting life and property during a flood.

WHAT ABOUT THE FUTURE?

Floods are usually caused by natural events, but damage to inhabited areas can be amplified by developers who are unaware of flood safety guidelines or choose to ignore them. They can change the course of rivers and build homes, factories, and entire communities in areas that are at high risk for floods. Developers may also build in coastal areas that are defenseless against high seas. Then the floods come at a tremendous cost.

Rowing down an Evanston, Illinois, street during the 1993 flood

The Midwest flood of 1993 awakened government officials, citizens, and flood experts to the possibility that conventional methods of flood control may not be sufficient. Many experts believe that some floodplains and wetlands should be restored to their natural condition. This action would increase habitats for wildlife and native plants that are adapted to floods. It would also solve some flood control problems by moving communities out of the areas that are at the highest risk for floods.

Some areas along the Mississippi River are already being considered for this kind of plan. The Federal Emergency Management Agency plans to purchase and demolish 8,000 homes in the Midwest floodplain. The agency will provide grants to local governments to convert the lands into open spaces. A study of the 1993 flood disaster recommends moving people out of risky areas as a means of flood control. In St. Charles County, Missouri, alone the federal government will spend 20 million dollars to buy 800 properties, including 300 mobile homes, in an effort to depopulate the area. More than 40 percent of this county lies in the floodplain.

Moving people out of the floodplain has the obvious benefit of protecting life, property, and the environment. It has another value. Each time a town is severely damaged by high water, much of the cost for disaster relief is paid with federal and state taxes. In the 1993 Midwest flood, less than 10 percent of the damaged homes were covered by flood insurance, even though many of these areas have been repeatedly flooded over the years. Only 50 percent of the affected farmers had crop insurance. This lack of

The inhabitants of St. Louis, Missouri, are committed to making life in the floodplain safe. Here, the St. Louis floodwall protects the city from the 1993 flood.

insurance increases the amount of state and federal funds that must be used. Since 1993, some taxpayers have expressed strong dissatisfaction concerning the repeated cost of bailing out flood victims who don't have flood insurance. These people often support relocation over rebuilding in the floodplain.

Relocation, however, also has a tremendous cost. It would disrupt the lives of a large number of people whose families have inhabited the floodplain for generations. For many, the thought of leaving the floodplain is far worse than the floods. For example, in St. Louis, Missouri, decaying riverfronts have been restored and turned into public parks and tourist attractions. Riverfront recreation includes boating, bird-watching, and fishing. The citizens of towns and cities such as St. Louis now want to preserve what they have and, in some instances, what they have lost.

The competing costs of relocation versus rebuilding have sparked intense debates about alternative flood management plans. Should agricultural fields be converted to wetlands? Should all the levees be rebuilt? Are the costs of floods greater than the costs of moving towns out of the floodplains?

In the United States, citizens are realizing that levees and dams do not always protect communities. Past flood reduction policies are not always adequate. But what is the best solution? Regardless of the answer, national, state, and local agencies must cooperate in their flood management policies. Public awareness now requires that flood risks be weighed carefully against the benefits of living and investing in flood-prone areas. The final analysis will be made in terms of human safety and the effects of floods on all of our lives.

FOR FURTHER READING

Clark, Champ. *Flood*. Alexandria, VA: Time-Life Books, 1982.

Fradin, Dennis B. *Floods*. Chicago: Children's Press, 1982.

Greenberg, Keith Elliot. *Hurricanes and Tornadoes*. New York: Twenty-First Century Books, 1994.

Lampton, Christopher. *Tidal Wave*. Brookfield, CT: Millbrook Press, 1992.

Lampton, Christopher. *Hurricane*. Brookfield, CT: Millbrook Press, 1991.

Oleksy, Walter G. *Nature Gone Wild!* New York: J. Messner, 1982.

Rozens, Aleksandrs, *Floods*. New York: Twenty-First Century Books, 1994.

Watson, Benjamin A. *Acts of God: The Old Farmer's Almanac Unpredictable Guide to Weather and Natural Disasters*. New York: Random House, 1993.

INTERNET RESOURCES

Due to the changeable nature of the Internet, sites appear and disappear very quickly. The resources listed below offered useful information on floods at the time of publication. Internet addresses must be entered with capital and lower-case letters exactly as they appear.

The *Yahoo* directory of the World Wide Web is an excellent place to find Internet sites on any topic. The directory is located at:

http://www.yahoo.com

The mission of the Federal Emergency Management Agency (FEMA) is "to provide leadership and support to reduce the loss of life and property and protect our nation's institutions from all types of hazards." FEMA publishes lots of flood related materials on its Web site. It is located at:

http://www.fema.gov

"The National Weather Service site lists all the areas across the country that are currently under watch or warning for thunderstorms, tornadoes, hurricanes, flash flooding, and other

climatic episodes" —*Newsweek,* December 11, 1995.
The site is located at:

http://www.nws.noaa.gov

The National Weather Service's Interactive Weather Information
Network (IWIN) can be reached directly at:

http://iwin.nws.noaa.gov/iwin/main.html

Satellite images such as the one on p. 34 can be viewed and
downloaded from the Goes Project Web site. The address is:

http://climate.gsfc.nasa.gov/~chesters/goesproject.html

INDEX

ABOUT THE AUTHOR

Ann Armbruster has been an English teacher and a school librarian. She is the author of Franklin Watts First Books: *The American Flag*, *The United Nations*, *Tornadoes*, and *Wildfires*. Ms. Armbruster lives in Cambridge, Ohio.